TREVOR WYE

Beginner's Book
for the *Flute*
PART TWO

Order No. NOV120585

Novello Publishing Limited

Illustrations by Gordon Davies A.R.A.

Cover by Art & Design

Exclusive distributors:
Hal Leonard
7777 West Bluemound Road, Milwaukee, WI 53213
Email: info@halleonard.com
Hal Leonard Europe Limited
42 Wigmore Street Maryleborne, London, WIU 2 RN
Email: info@halleonardeurope.com Hal Leonard Australia Pty. Ltd.
4 Lentara Court Cheltenham, Victoria, 9132 Australia
Email: info@halleonard.com.au

Also available from Novello:

PLAY THE FLUTE: a beginner's guide
A Novello Video (Colour: 35 minutes)
Presented by Trevor Wye
Order No: NOV 640001

This innovative video is intended to be a self-contained guide to the fundamentals of flute playing, but students are sure to benefit from the use of the video in conjunction with the publication on which it is based, A Beginner's Book for the Flute (Part 1, Part 2 and Piano Accompaniments).

Also available from Novello:

A Practice Book for the Flute by Trevor Wye

This highly successful series of Practice Books for the Flute has proved to be of tremendous value to players of all grades from beginners to advanced students. Each book has a dependence upon the others and concentrates on an individual facet of flute playing in detail. Collectively they form a broad reference to the technical difficulties of the instrument, without concentrating on any one particular method of study.

The six volumes deal with:

Volume 1　TONE
Volume 2　TECHNIQUE
Volume 3　ARTICULATION
Volume 4　INTONATION AND VIBRATO
Volume 5　BREATHING AND SCALES
Volume 6　ADVANCED PRACTICE

For Kate Hill

PREFACE

Any new book appearing on the market usually boasts of new ideas and new format. This book is no different in this respect though it does incorporate all the well-tried recipes of the past.

Technically, the flute is the easiest of the woodwind instruments and one which lends itself most readily to being learnt chromatically. It is easier for a beginner to play in different keys, provided that the learning of each new note is given equal emphasis.

The general outline of this book is, therefore, to encourage:
  (a) enjoyment of flute playing and music making in the broadest sense.
  (b) familiarity with the lesser-known keys which, in turn, results in easier access to orchestras and ensembles.
  (c) the formation of a firm low register, the foundation to a good tone throughout the compass of the flute.
  (d) solo and ensemble playing.

The 72 numbered pieces (1-42 are in PART I, the rest in PART II) in this book can mostly be played either:
  1) as a solo
  2) as a duet
  3) as a solo with piano
  4) as a duet with piano
  5) as a solo or duet with guitar accompaniment.

The book of piano accompaniments, in which chord symbols are given, are up to Grade VI (Associated Board) in standard (though many are easier), and is available separately.

The book is intended for both individual and group tuition. It can be used without a teacher if circumstances make this necessary though a pupil is strongly advised to consult a good teacher.

Many exercises and tunes are by the author.

Piano accompaniments by Robert Scott with nine original pieces specially composed by Alan Ridout.

Finally, I acknowledge with grateful thanks, the players and teachers who have advised me on the preparation of this book:

Lucy Cartledge, Catharine Hill, Malcolm Pollack, Rosemary Rathbone, Alastair Roberts, Lenore Smith, Robin Soldan, Hilary Taggart, Stephanie Tromans, Lindsay Winfield-Chislett and Janet Way.

TREVOR WYE

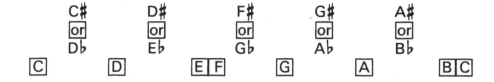

NEW NAMES FOR OLD NOTES

This diagram looks like a row of houses, some of which are semi-detached and some, detached. Some houses have garages between them. The garage between G and A is shared by both of them therefore, that garage could be called G sharp or A flat.

For reasons which will be clearer later, all notes have more than one name. The note (or garage) between C and D is *either* C which has been sharpened or D which has been made flat.

Between B and C and between E and F there is no garage. If we want to call F by another name then it is called E sharp; similarly E is F flat.

First study the diagram then cover it up and write *another* name for each of the notes listed here:

For example:

A♯	=	B♭	B♯	=	.....
E♯	=	F	G♭	=	.....
G♭	=	F♯	E♭	=	.....
F♯	=	.....	B	=	.....
F♭	=	.....	E	=	.....
A♭	=	.....	D♭	=	.....
A♯	=	.....	C♯	=	.....
D♯	=	.....	C	=	.....
B♭	=	.....	G♯	=	.....
F	=	.....			

The next exercises are chromatic (from a Greek word meaning all colours). When playing them try not to 'translate' notes (i.e. from A♭ to G♯). It will help you to read at sight.

E minor

43

THE AQUARIUM

SAINT-SAENS

Lento

A CHROMATIC SCALE

$\frac{2}{2}$ time is two minin beats in a bar.

D minor

Moderato

rall.

E minor

44

THE ACROBAT

Mesto (sadly)

rall.

56

A VERY SAD TUNE

An exercise and piece in F sharp minor:

SCALE EXERCISE IN F♯ MINOR

HYMN

J. PARRY

MARCH

ALAN RIDOUT

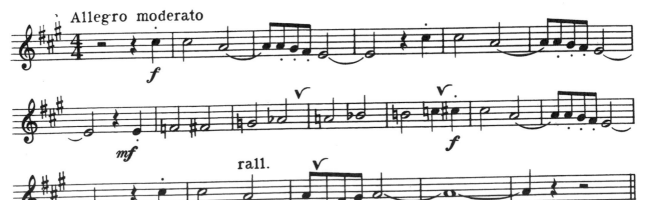

Compound time

When the *pulse* or *beat* can be divided into three, the music is said to be in compound time.
⁶⁄₈ time is one example. There are two dotted crotchet beats in each bar. Each dotted crotchet
has three quavers. Ex. 1: count two beats in a bar; in bars 3 and 4 think the word 'COVENTRY'
to help you play the correct rhythm. Ex. 2: bars 2 and 3 should sound exactly the same.

I SAW THREE SHIPS

G major

Moderato

C major

48

SOEUR MONIQUE

COUPERIN

Andante

p

rall. 2nd time

Introducing upper G sharp or A flat

Check the tuning of your octaves.

A flat major: four flats: B♭ , E♭ , A♭ and D♭ .

SCALE EXERCISE IN A♭ MAJOR

A♭ major

49   PLAISIR D'AMOUR

MARTINI

SCALE EXERCISE IN E♭ MAJOR

E♭ major

FIFERS CALL

E♭ major

18th century

60

Sometimes the time-signature changes during a piece, but as in this example, the pulse or beat remains the same. $\frac{3}{8}$ is equal to half a bar of $\frac{6}{8}$.

HUNTING SONG

G major

FRENCH
18th century

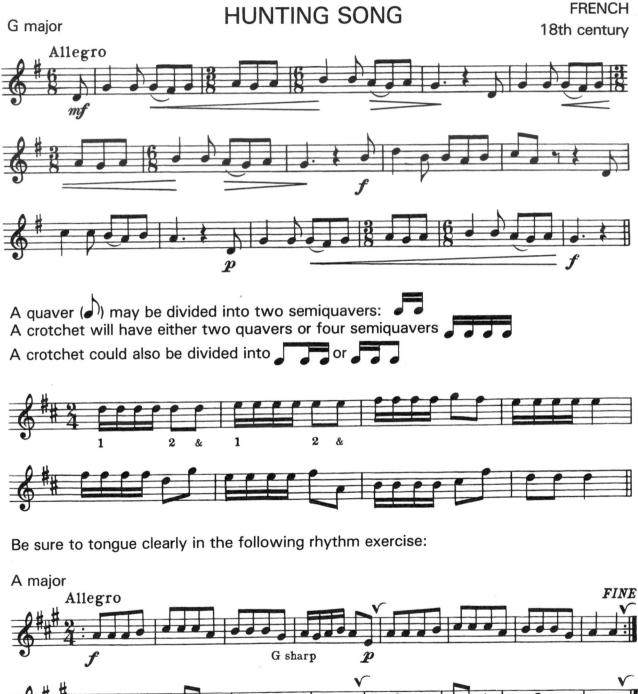

A quaver (♪) may be divided into two semiquavers:
A crotchet will have either two quavers or four semiquavers
A crotchet could also be divided into ♩ or ♩

Be sure to tongue clearly in the following rhythm exercise:

A major

D minor

Dotted quavers

First, play this exercise quickly, two beats in a bar

G major

DOT'S TUNE

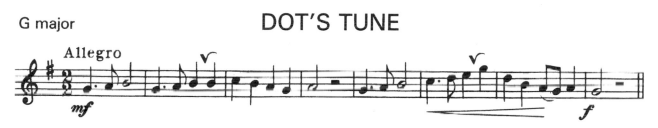

This next exercise *sounds* the same as the one above. Think of the rhythm to the words 'once a-gain'.

DOT'S TUNE

G major

50

GAVOTTE

A. CORELLI

A minor

GREENSLEEVES

A triplet
When three notes are played in the same time as two notes of the same value, they are called a triplet. The three quavers below are played in the time of two quavers. A triplet is marked by the figure 3 above or below the three notes.

D minor

Grace notes
These are added to a melody to decorate it. They are always written in small print, and are played quickly.

G major

51

FANTASY PIECE

SCHUMANN

Introducing upper A, B and C

C major
52

THE HARVESTERS

COUPERIN

Tone Exercise: refer to the earlier comments before playing these exercises. Use a firm support of the air stream. They should be practised every day: Tone practice is not a Sunday pastime.

TONE EXERCISE

C# minor

53

LAMENT

ALAN RIDOUT

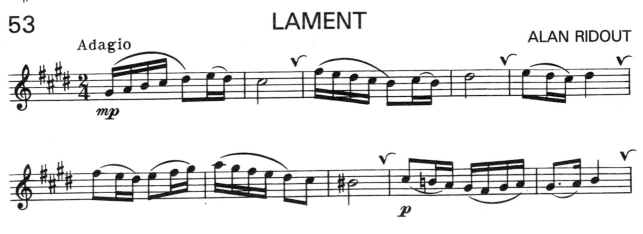

Introducing upper B flat or A sharp

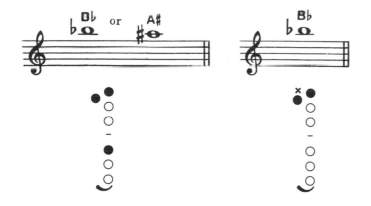

B♭ is sometimes, in fast passages, fingered with the thumb on the B♭ lever.

See diagram in the front of PART I.

SCALE EXERCISE IN F MAJOR

Notice of a flute and piano duet, played by Miss Banks and the Rev. Mr Mayhew. (19th century)

"After an adagio opening, in which the flute and piano were at magnificent cross purposes from the beginning, the two instruments plunged into an allegro, very long and very fast, which became ultimately a desperate race between the competing performers for the final chord. The shriller and wilder grew the flute, and the greater exertion of the Hercules performing upon it, the fiercer grew the pace of the piano. *Crash*, came the last chord, and the poor flute nearly half a page behind, was left shrilly hanging in mid air, forsaken and companionless, an object of derision to gods and men."

Mrs Ward

F major

54

DANCE

V. HAUPTMANN

$\frac{9}{8}$ is another compound time: three dotted crotchet beats in each bar.

FOLK SONG

Bb major

TRADITIONAL

SCALE EXERCISE IN E MAJOR

SWEDISH FOLK SONG

E major

SCALE EXERCISE IN A MAJOR

Metronome marks

A metronome is a mechanical or electrical device which gives the beat or speed of a piece of music. For example, you will see at the start of a piece, ♩ = 120. This indicates that there are one hundred and twenty crotchets to the minute. If a metronome is not available, think of the beat of a brisk military march: there are about 120 beats to the minute, and half of that will give 60 beats to the minute or one per second.

Most watches give 5 ticks per second, therefore, every fifth tick is a beat of 60 to the minute. Every fourth tick is therefore, 75 to the minute, every 3rd, 100 to the minute and every 2nd, 150 to the minute. A little practice, and patience, will soon give a fairly accurate guide to the speed of a piece.

Note that it is not always the beat which is indicated but sometimes a note value such as ♩ = 90 in **3/4** time.

68

A major
55

MINUET

J.S. BACH

rall. 2nd time

Introducing C sharp and C

C♯ and C, the lowest notes on the flute, are rather more difficult.

Use the tone exercise below to gain strength in these notes.

Moderato

Allegro

Acciaccatura
A long name for a very short note: it is played on the beat and as short as possible.

Bb major

G minor

56   BALLET   RAMEAU

TONE EXERCISE FOR THE LOW NOTES

SCALE EXERCISE IN C MINOR

C minor

BASS DANCE

57

ARBEAU-WARLOCK

Animato (animated) ♩ = 120

Syncopation

When the pulse or beat falls in the *middle* of a note, it is said to be syncopated. Syncopation usually adds a bouncy, dance quality to a piece. The second tune should sound the same as the first tune.

1   Moderato ♩ = 72

2   Moderato ♩ = 72

C major

SCOTCH DANCE

58

BEETHOVEN

Allegretto ♩ = 90

F major
MILONGA
59 Moderato ♩ = 80

SOUTH AMERICAN

SCALE EXERCISE IN C♯ MINOR

C♯ minor

Andante ♪ = 90

72

Bars' rest
Sometimes pieces of music contain bars' rests: they are shown by |⎯⎯⎯⎯| with the appropriate figure above them:

12
|⎯⎯⎯⎯|

In this instance the piano has a one bar introduction.

G major

60 NEAPOLITAN AIR

ANON.

B minor
61

ANDANTE

ALAN RIDOUT

Introducing top C sharp and D

SCALE EXERCISE IN D MAJOR

D major
62

SICILIENNE

VIVALDI

Larghetto ♪ = 112

SCALE EXERCISE IN D MINOR

BASS DANCE

D minor

WALTZ

Db major

SCHUBERT

C# minor

A student was playing the flute
When it fell and stuck in his boot
In spite of his strength
He exclaimed, at length
'For the rest of my life, I'll be mute'!

Introducing top E

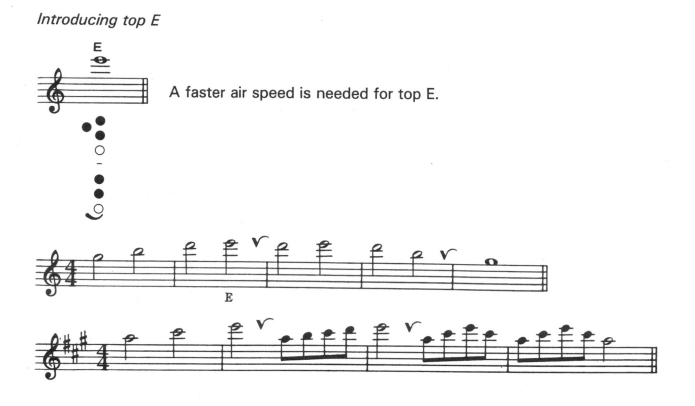

A faster air speed is needed for top E.

G major

QUEM PASTORES

63

14th century

Grazioso ♩=108

* Trill

Another decoration: let your third finger bounce three or four times on the key to rapidly alternate F♯ and G for the duration of the note. Trills always go upwards, the note above being the next one up according to the key-signature.

SCALE EXERCISE IN A MINOR

CANON FOR TWO

Player II starts when player I is on the second note.

A minor

MENDELSSOHN

A major

64

ROSAMUNDE

SCHUBERT

78

Introducing top E flat and F

SCALE EXERCISE IN B♭ MAJOR

B♭ major

65

ANDANTE

SCHUBERT

Andante ♩ = 66

p dolce (sweetly)

mf

cresc.

f

C major

66

AIR

J. CLINTON

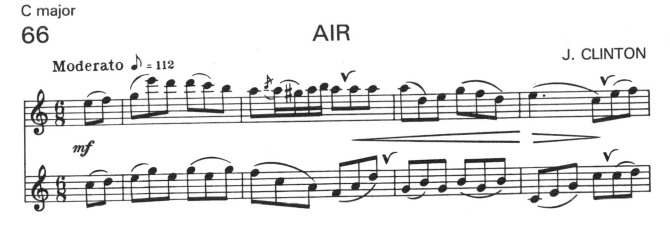

G minor

67

LANE'S TUNE

PLAYFORD (1695)

Con spirito (with spirit) ♩ = 72

rall. last time

FINE

D.C. al Fine

6 Theobold Boehm in his workshop making a flute. He was the inventor of the flute you play which has remained unchanged since 1847. Boehm was a fine flute player, composer and silversmith. He died in 1881 at the age of seventy-eight.

Tone Exercises
These can be found in *The Practice Books for the Flute Volume I* – TONE published by
NOVELLO which contains comprehensive exercises for all tone problems.

F# major
68

BARCAROLLE

ALAN RIDOUT

Introducing top F sharp and G

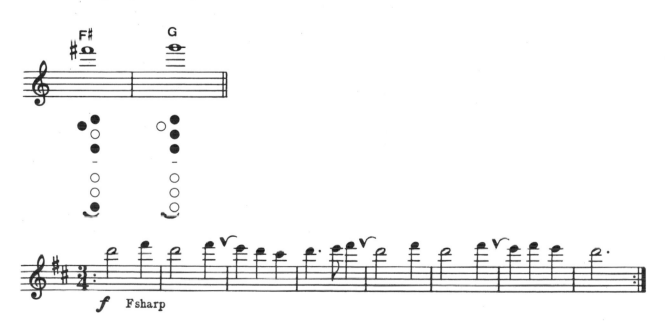

7 Franz Doppler and his younger brother Carl caused 'quite a sensation all over Europe' around 1850 by the way in which they played duets beautifully together. Carl played the flute on the left of his body, a practice once quite common but which has now died out. It is not possible to play in this way on modern flutes.

G major

MINUET

J. S. BACH

69 Tempo di minuetto (in minuet time) ♩ = 120

SCALE EXERCISE IN A♭ MAJOR

A♭ major

70   PIEDS EN L'AIR

ARBEAU-WARLOCK

An odd duet: the 2nd player starts at the end and plays backwards!

A minor

CANON

FIRST PART

J. S. BACH

Moderato ♩ = 96

SECOND PART

D major

HUNTING THE HARE

TRADITIONAL

Scale and arpeggio requirements for the Associated Board, Grade 3, flute; to be played both tongued and slurred.

A minor

86

Introducing top G sharp or A flat, and A

A flat

A

SCALE EXERCISE IN A MAJOR

Books of exercises for both finger technique and articulation are recommended at this stage, in addition to the Tone Book:

A Trevor Wye Practice Book for the Flute.
 Volume I   Tone
 Volume II   Technique
 Volume III   Articulation
 Volume IV   Intonation and Vibrato
 Volume V   Breathing and Scales

published by Novello.

C major

71

RIGADOON

RAMEAU

The drum and the vile squeeking of the wry-neck't fife.

SHAKESPEARE (Merchant of Venice)

A Grand Final piece with seven variations which uses some of the techniques learnt in this book.

E minor

GRAND FINALE
MINUET WITH VARIATIONS

72

J.J. QUANTZ
freely arranged by T.W.

THEME

Repeat the second part throughout all variations.

VARIATION I

VARIATION II

VARIATION III

VARIATION IV

VARIATION V

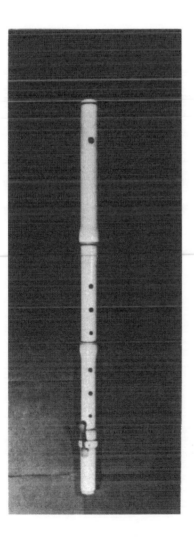

Knaves are men that lute and flute fantastic tenderness

TENNYSON (The Princess)

The one-keyed flute. This was the flute used from about 1720. More keys were added between that date and 1830 when Theobald Boehm (see page 80) began his experiments. It has been recently revived, and can be heard at concerts today where it is usually called the Baroque flute, or Flauto Traverso.

VARIATION VI

VARIATION VII

Why not write a variation or two of your own on the manuscript provided on pages 94 and 95.

The fingering of these last three notes is for future reference.

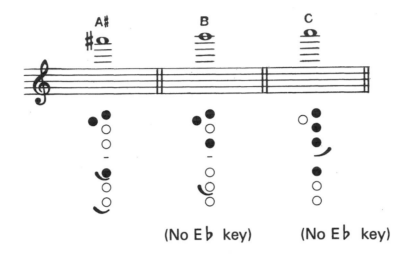

(No E♭ key)   (No E♭ key)

A list of Italian words and their meanings

Allegro	quickly
Allegretto	less quickly than Allegro
Andante	slowly
Andantino	less slow than Andante, though some composers use it to mean less *fast* (or slower), than Andante. Use your own judgment.
A tempo	in the original time (after slowing down)
Animato	animated
Al fine	to the finish (after D.C.)
Con spirito	with spirit
Crescendo (cresc.)	gradually getting louder
Con	with
Con moto	with motion
Diminuendo (dim.)	gradually getting softer
Dolce	sweetly
D.C. (da capo)	go back to the beginning
Fine	the finish
Forte (f)	loudly
Grazioso	gracefully
Larghetto	less slow than largo
Maestoso	majestically
Mezzo forte (mf)	half, or moderately loud
Mezzo piano (mp)	half, or moderately soft
Mesto	sadly
Moderato	at a moderate speed
Ritenuto (rit.)	holding back
Rallentando (rall.)	gradually getting slower
Sostenuto	sustained
Simile	continue in the same way
Tempo	time
Tempo di minuetto	in a minuet time
Tempo di Valse	in waltz time
Vivo	very quickly and lively
Vivace	lively

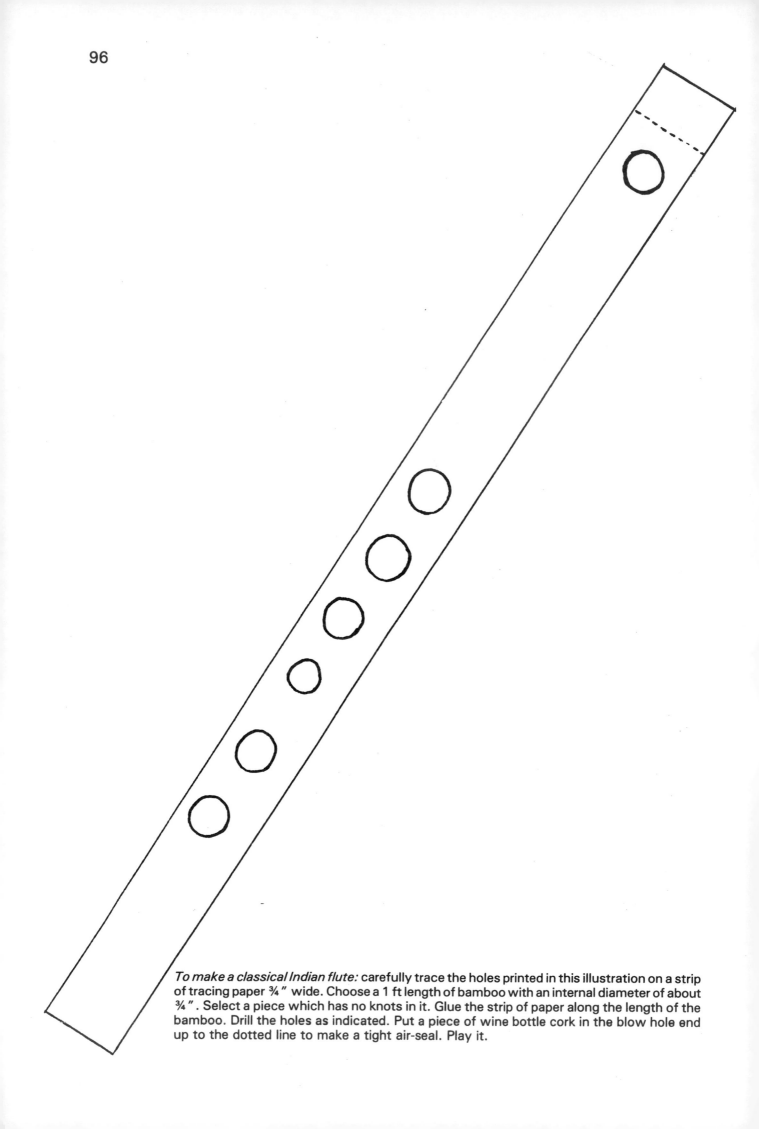

To make a classical Indian flute: carefully trace the holes printed in this illustration on a strip of tracing paper ¾" wide. Choose a 1 ft length of bamboo with an internal diameter of about ¾". Select a piece which has no knots in it. Glue the strip of paper along the length of the bamboo. Drill the holes as indicated. Put a piece of wine bottle cork in the blow hole end up to the dotted line to make a tight air-seal. Play it.

APPENDIX

Scale and arpeggio requirements for the Associated Board, Grade 3; to be played both tongued and slurred.

GRADE 3

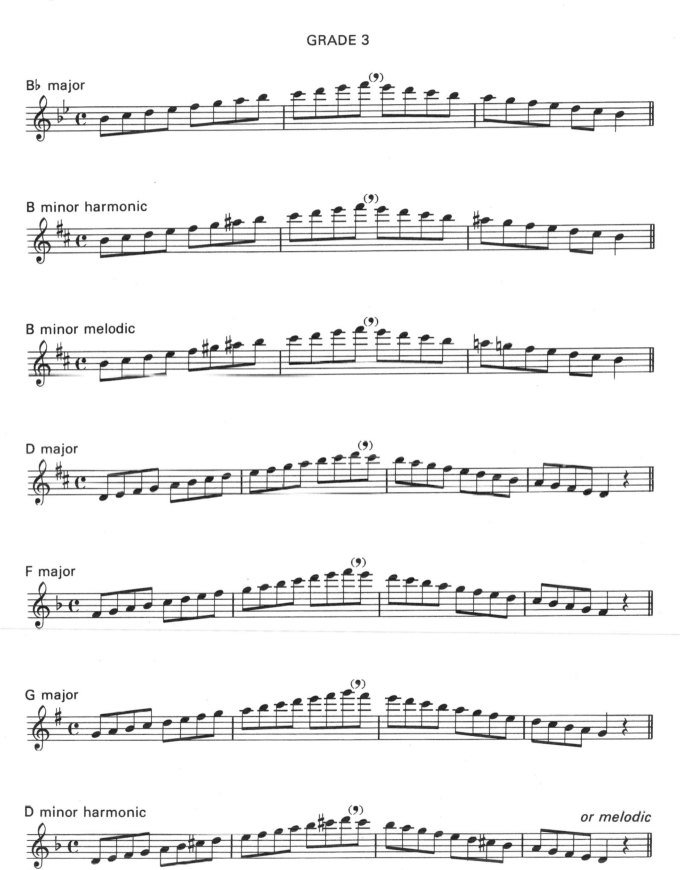

E minor harmonic

or melodic

G minor harmonic

or melodic

Chromatic

B♭ major   **B minor**

D major   **F major**

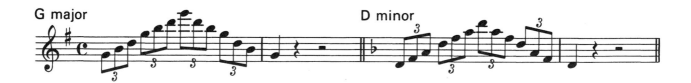

G major   **D minor**

E minor   **G minor**